NEVER FAILS

By Kenneth E. Hagin

Chapter 1
LOVE: THE FIRST FRUIT
OF THE SPIRIT

But the fruit of the Spirit is love, joy, peace, longsuffering, gentleness, goodness, faith,

Meekness, temperance: against such there is no law.

— Galatians 5:22,23

As W. E. Vine and others point out, this passage in Galatians is not referring to the Holy Spirit; it's referring to the human spirit, although the Holy Spirit is involved.

At times it's difficult to tell whether Paul is talking about the Holy Spirit or the human spirit because the same Greek word, *pneuma,* is used.

If you read the entire passage, however, you'll see that Paul is contrasting the works of the flesh with the works of the spirit. Verse 19 says, *"Now the works of the flesh are . . . ."* and verse 22 continues, *"But the fruit of the Spirit is . . . ."*

So this passage actually refers to the fruit of the recreated, born-again human spirit. Of course, this comes about because of the life of Christ — the Holy Spirit — within.

Now let's turn to the fifteenth chapter of John's Gospel and notice what Jesus says:

JOHN 15:1-5

1 I am the true vine, and my Father is the husbandman.

2 Every branch in me that beareth not fruit he taketh away [I wonder what fruit He meant we were to bear?]: and every branch that beareth fruit, he purgeth it, that it may bring forth more fruit.

3 Now ye are clean through the word which I have spoken unto you.

4 Abide in me, and I in you. As the branch cannot bear fruit of itself, except it abide in the vine; no more can ye, except ye abide in me.

5 I am the vine, ye are the branches: He that abideth in me, and I in him, the same bringeth forth much fruit: for without me ye can do nothing.

Jesus is using a tree as an example: "*I am the vine, ye are the branches . . . .*" Where does fruit grow? Fruit grows on the branches, doesn't it? Yet the branch cannot produce fruit of itself. Cut a branch off the tree and see how much fruit it produces. That branch produces fruit *because of* the life — the sap — that comes up through the tree and into the branches.

Therefore, this "fruit of the spirit" is

not *entirely* the fruit of the Holy Spirit; it is the fruit that grows in our life. It is the fruit of the recreated, born-again human spirit through the life of Christ within.

Notice that *the first fruit of the spirit is love.* That's the first fruit that shows up in the recreated, born-again human spirit.

Now let's look at the First Epistle of John: *"We know that we have passed from death unto life . . . ."* (1 John 3:14). John is not talking about physical death here; he's talking about spiritual death. This verse means that we have passed from spiritual death unto spiritual life. It's another way of saying we know we're saved — born again.

How do we know it? *"We know that we have passed from death unto life, BECAUSE WE LOVE THE BRETHREN. He that loveth not his brother abideth in death"* (v. 14).

Now turn back to John's Gospel:

JOHN 13:34,35
34 A new commandment I give unto you, That ye

love one another; as I have loved you, that ye also love one another.
35 By this shall all men know that ye are my disciples, if ye have love one to another.

The natural human being can't do that. He can't love the one who is unconverted unless he's been born again. When you're born again, the Holy Spirit resides within your spirit. Romans 5:5 says, "...*the love of God* [the God-kind of love] *is shed abroad in our hearts* [or spirits] *by the Holy Ghost....*" Hallelujah! Therefore, you see, we can love *even as He loved,* because we have the same kind of love in us that He had in Him!

You have to realize that because *fruit grows,* you should mature in all areas of your Christian walk, but love is the first fruit that will show up in your spirit and life once you are born again.

You see, to fellowship with God — to walk in God's realm — we must walk in love, for God is love. This is not natural human love, it is divine love, the love of God.

When you and I became born again, God became our Father. He is a love God. We are love children of a love God, because we have been born of God, and God is love. The nature of God in us is love. We have His nature in our spirit, not in our flesh. (We've got the flesh to contend with, but we can "crucify" it.)

And we can't say we don't have this divine love, because everybody in the family of God has it — or else they're not in the family. They may not be exercising it, but they have it. We need to continue to feed that love nature of ours on the Word, exercise it, and it will grow. *You can grow in love.*

We see in First John 4:18, *"There is no fear in love; but perfect love casteth out fear...."* I haven't seen anybody who's been made perfect in love yet, have you? But, praise God, some of us are on our way, and we're going to stay after it and keep growing.

Let me repeat this because it's so important: Everybody in the family of God has this divine love. Paul said, writing to the Church at Ephesus, *"For this cause I bow my knees unto the Father of our Lord Jesus Christ, Of whom the WHOLE family in heaven and earth is named . . . ."* (Eph. 3:14,15). We can say this family is the love family, because it's the family of God, and God is love. You can't say you don't have love, because if you say you don't, you're saying you haven't been born again.

I remember one time I was holding a meeting in a Full Gospel church in California. Other ministers visited the morning teaching class. One day several of us, along with the pastor, went out for a noon meal. While they were talking, I just sat and listened. They were talking about this very subject: love.

"That's what we need — we need a revival of love. We need a baptism of love. We need to pray about it," some of them said. Finally the pastor asked, "What do you say about it, Brother Hagin?"

I replied, "Well, if all you fellows need love, you all ought to get saved!"

If they'd been wearing false teeth, they would have swallowed them!

I continued, "The Bible says in Romans 5:5 that the love of God has been shed abroad in our hearts by the Holy Ghost. The Bible says we know we've passed from death unto life because we love.

"Now, if you haven't been born again, you don't have that love in you. But we have that divine love, and it can grow and be developed because fruit grows. So you don't need to pray for love; you need to confess that the love of God is in you. You need to keep feeding it on the Word of God and keep exercising it, and you'll develop and grow in love."

They began to see that. They said, "We were all wrong. We were about to pray to God to give us a revival of love, and we've already got it!"

Often we're praying for things that are already ours. What we need to do is recognize whatever it is we need, confess it, believe it, walk in the light of it, and exercise it, and we'll develop it.

Natural human love is selfish. It is concerned about *me,* what is *mine,* what *I* can have, and what *I* have to put up with. Divine love is unselfish. It is not concerned with how I can use you and what I can get from you. It is concerned with what I can give. Oh, how the Church needs to know and walk in the light of divine love! It will solve your problems for you.

Human love will turn to hatred overnight. That is the reason so many married persons say, "I just don't love him (or her) anymore." They are operating entirely on natural human love when they say that.

Divine love (when both husband and wife were operating in divine love) never has been to the divorce court. Natural love has.

Chapter 2
LOVE INCLUDES
MOTHERS-IN-LAW

One night after a church service, my wife and I went out to eat with the pastor and his wife. This pastor's wife said, "Brother Hagin, you've got me in a mess. Since I've heard you preach, I don't even know if I'm saved or not!"

I knew she grew up in a Full Gospel parsonage, was graduated from a Full Gospel Bible school, and both she and her husband were ordained ministers.

"How did I confuse you?" I asked.

She explained that one night I had quoted from First John 3:15, which says, *"Whosoever hateth his brother is a murderer; and ye know that no murderer hath eternal life abiding in him."* I had added, "And that includes mothers-in-law."

This woman said, "I hate my mother-in-law!"

I said, "Well, if that's the case, then of course you *aren't* saved. You *don't* have eternal life in you." (I was going to rescue her in a moment, but I wanted her to see herself, so I let her stew for a while.)

I knew what the problem was; it is a problem for many Christians. They really do not know what they have or who they are in Christ. They let their mind (unrenewed with the Word of God) or their flesh (which is unsanctified) confuse them, and that can really get them into a mess.

I decided to rescue this sister. I said, "Look me in the eye and say, 'I hate my mother-in-law.' At the same time, check down in your spirit (not up in your brain). What happens in there?"

She looked across the table and said, "I hate my mother-in-law."

"Now," I said, "what happened down on the inside of you?"

She said, "There is something down there 'scratching' me."

I said, "I know it. It is the love of God

that has been shed abroad in your heart trying to get your attention."

"What should I do?" she asked.

I said, "Let that love that's on the inside of you dominate you. Don't let your thinking dominate you. I don't care what your head says. Your head sometimes can say some awful things. Don't let your flesh dominate you. Crucify the flesh. It hurts, but crucify it. Act from your heart. Act like you would if you *did* love her — *because you really do.*"

A few days later, she came to me and said, "You know, you are exactly right. I don't hate my mother-in-law. I don't hate my husband's family. They're good people. They're Christians. They love the Lord."

It's easy to get in the flesh if you are not careful. I could understand it in this case. This woman's husband was the only son of a widow who had never let him go.

I don't care if people are saved and filled with the Holy Spirit: If they don't get into the Word and let the love of God dominate them, they will walk in the natural. But thank God, the love of God has been shed abroad in our hearts by the Holy Spirit.

If we could just get people to walk in love and know what belongs to them *because* they're walking in love, we wouldn't have to have healing services for Christians! We'd have them for unbelievers instead.

Let's look again at John 13:35: *"By this shall all men* [That's everybody, isn't it?] *know that ye are my disciples, if ye have love one to another."*

Isn't it strange how easily we get into error? Some say, "They're going to know that you're disciples because you adhere to all these laws, bylaws, and principles." No — if you have love one to another.

How does God love us?

JOHN 13:34
34 A new commandment I give unto you, That ye love one another; AS I HAVE LOVED YOU, that ye also love one another.

That's the love law that belongs to the family of God.

Did God love us because we deserved it? No, He loved us while we were unlovely. He loved us while we were still sinners! The Bible says so:

ROMANS 5:8
8 But God commendeth his love toward us, in that, while we were yet sinners, Christ died for us.

Think about this: If God loved us with such a great love when we were sinners — unlovely — His enemies — do you think He loves His children any *less?* No, a thousand times no! That's the way we're to love with divine love. This love that the Bible is talking about is divine love — the God-kind of love — the love of God that has been shed abroad in our hearts by the Holy Spirit.

We hear a lot today about "love," but what people are really talking about is natural human love, which is selfish. Some say that a mother's love is like the love of

God. There may be similarities, but it's still natural love.

Often when a mother has just one son, she thinks there's no girl in all the world who's good enough for him. That's natural love — that's not the love of God. And sometimes if Dad's not careful, particularly if he's got just one daughter, he thinks there's no boy in the world good enough for his girl.

As a usual thing, a mother's love is human — and it's selfish. "That's *my* baby," mothers say. "Those are *my* children." Yes, they are, but you ought to teach those children that the time's coming when they're going to have to cut mother's apron strings.

Jesus Himself referred to it. In discussing marriage, He said that in the beginning God said a man was to forsake his mother and father for his wife. He didn't mean to forsake them in the modern sense of the word. It simply means, "Don't live with your in-laws!" You're going against the Bible if you do. Now I realize certain situations arise when a couple might have to live with in-laws temporarily. My wife and I did when we first got married. But don't live with them for very long!

Somebody will complain, "Well, we just can't make it otherwise."

Yes, you can. Believe God!

And it's the same with the wife as it is with the husband. When a couple has their own dwelling, there's no mother-in-law to boss the situation. You're getting on unscriptural grounds when you don't leave mother and father and cleave to your spouse (Gen. 2:24; Matt. 19:4-6). I could really do some meddling here!

If we'd just follow the Bible, it would solve all of our problems!

Chapter 3
HUMAN VS. DIVINE LOVE

The pianist for one of my meetings was a young woman who played beautifully. I learned from the pastor that she had graduated with a degree in music from a university in that city.

But when you'd look at her, she'd duck her head. She acted strangely.

I asked the pastor, "Is she completely normal?"

"Oh, it's a sad situation, Brother Hagin," he said. "She was graduated from the university here and she could teach music, but she doesn't do anything. Her mother has held her right to her coattails. She's never had a girlfriend or boyfriend in her life."

This girl was about 27 years old. She had never spent one night away from home. The pastor also told me that the girl had three brothers. Their mother, a widow, never let any of them visit a friend's house overnight or have a friend spend the night with them. They had no friends.

A person's personality becomes twisted in such cases. That's not love, friends. That's natural human love, and it's selfish. It's what *I* want, not what you need or want.

The boys respected their mother, but as soon as they finished high school, they left home. During the time I was there in the meeting, the last boy, who had just graduated at 17, left home. He didn't say anything to his mother; he just left.

She came to me bawling. "Brother Hagin, I want you to pray. So-and-so's gone. Now, he's a good boy — saved and filled with the Holy Ghost — but he's not honoring his mother. I want you to pray about it."

I said, "What for?"

"Well, he's left."

I said, "Thank God!"

She looked at me like I'd slapped her with a wet dish rag.

I said, "I'm so glad he had enough sense to get out of that mess."

She began to cry. She said, "I love my children."

I said, "No, you don't. Look at that poor girl on the piano. Dear Lord, she can play all right — she has musical ability — but when you look at her she'll look down as if something's wrong with her. You kept her close to you all of her life. She never had a friend. She never spent one night away from home. You never let her out of your sight. She ought to be out on her own."

I added, "Instead of praying he'll come back, I'm going to pray that she'll leave."

"Oh, I love my children," the woman said.

"I know it," I said. "You love them with natural love. You're saved. Why don't you start loving them with the love of God? If you'd love them with the love of God, you'd be glad for them to leave home. They're old enough to go."

Natural love is selfish, but divine love is unselfish. A human being exercising natural human love is concerned about himself or herself, thinking, *What's in it for me?* We see this even in the Christian realm. Saved people — even ministers of the Gospel — may get in the natural and think this way.

Brother, we ought to be glad for the kingdom of God. The family of God is one. We ought to let the unselfish love of God dominate us.

Much of the time we don't walk in divine love, but we should. The love of God has been shed abroad in our hearts, and the first fruit of the spirit is love. We should be responding to that indwelling Spirit, shouldn't we?

Many churches have been torn up by people arguing, "Well, I've got my say — and I'm going to have it, too!" If they were to act in love, they just might keep their mouths shut.

The fruit of the spirit is love. That's

what God wants to reproduce in our recreated, born-again spirits because of the life of Christ and the Holy Spirit within.

What are the characteristics of the God-kind of love that has been shed abroad in our hearts? God didn't leave us in the dark. The Psalmist of old said, *"The entrance of thy words giveth light...."* (Ps. 119:130).

Now let's go to the thirteenth chapter of First Corinthians. It's to be regretted that the translators of the *King James Version* translated the Greek word for divine love, *agape,* as "charity." I don't think we understand exactly what Paul is saying here about "charity."

My favorite translation of this discourse on divine love is from *The Amplified Bible.* It starts with the fourth verse of First Corinthians 13:

"Love [divine love, the love of God] *endures long...."* But some say, "I'm not going to put up with that anymore. I've had it up to *here!"* That's the natural talk-

ing, isn't it? "*Love endures long and is patient and kind . . . .*" That has to be divine love. Many people endure long, all right, because they have to. Others say, "I've suffered all I'm going to. I'm not going to have it this way anymore." That's natural human love talking. God's love endures *long* and is patient and kind.

The verse continues, ". . .*love never is envious nor boils over with jealousy* [natural human love is jealous]; *is not boastful or vainglorious, does not display itself haughtily.*"

Verse 5 continues, "*It is not conceited — arrogant and inflated with pride; it is not rude (unmannerly), and does not act unbecomingly. Love [God's love in us] does not insist on its own rights or its own way, for it is not self-seeking; it is not touchy or fretful or resentful; it takes no account of the evil done to it — pays no attention to a suffered wrong.*"

When we read Scriptures like that, we don't shout too much. Take time to let that soak in. You see, so many people say, "Well, yes, but I know what's mine. I've got my rights, and I'm going to have them, no matter how much it might hurt somebody else."

Notice that it says *"Love does not insist on its own rights . . . ."* We'll never develop spiritually like God wants us to until we start believing God. That means believing His Word. That means believing that God's love is God's way — and that is the best way. And because it's God's way and the best way, it's your way.

The "love thermometer" or "love gauge" is found in this fifth verse: *"Love . . . is not touchy or fretful or resentful; it takes no account of the evil done to it — pays no attention to a suffered wrong."*

It's easy to find out whether or not we're walking in love. Just gauge yourself by what it says here about love. If you take account of the evil done to you, you're not walking in love. As long as you walk in love and stay full of the Holy Spirit, you won't take account of the evil done to you.

Chapter 4
THE LOVE CHAPTER

I have suggested for years that if you own an *Amplified Bible* turn to these verses from First Corinthians 13:4-8 every morning when you first get up and every night before you go to bed. Start confessing, "That's me. The love of God is in me."

You'll change so much that your family will ask, "Is that the same man (or woman)?" You will change so much that your spouse will almost think you're a different person.

Through the years, relatives or close friends have said to me, "They sure told you off, didn't they?"

I have replied, "No, they didn't tell me off. I take no account of evil. I wouldn't even take time to deny it if they claimed I'd killed my grandma. I'd just walk in love, praise God, keep the victory, and keep shouting.

Many years ago when I was pastoring,

a woman started a rumor about me. She told people she had seen Brother Hagin down on the railroad tracks with another woman at 4 o'clock in the morning.

Well, in the first place, what in the world was *she* doing out on the railroad tracks at 4 o'clock in the morning? (The devil will give himself away.)

I remember my wife and I were sitting in our living room when one of the women from the church came by all concerned because this tale was circulating about the pastor. She said, "This woman is telling that she saw Brother Hagin down on the railroad tracks with another woman at 4 o'clock in the morning!"

I didn't even respond. I began laughing. I tell you, I laughed so hard I had to get down on the floor! (When I get *really* tickled, I have to kick or roll — one of the two — so I just fell onto the floor rolling and laughing, I was so amused!) There was no truth to that rumor. But I didn't get into a fight with the woman who started it. I just forgave her and went on. And the rumor never got off the ground.

Through the years, when these things have happened to me, fellow pastors as well as relatives have told me, "I wouldn't take that if I were you. I wouldn't put up with that! Not me!"

I've even had pastors tell me I must have a weakness in my character because I wouldn't take any account of evil done to me — I'd just go along and act like nothing had been said or done against me. And I'd treat the person who did me an injustice just as well as I did anybody else.

But it's not a weakness; it's a strength! I just let something on the inside of me dominate me, and I really didn't know what it was until I got *The Amplified Bible* and read where it says that love takes no account of the evil done to it. Then I saw that it was a strength, because love never fails.

Many have failed — many have died prematurely — because they lived so much in the natural that they couldn't take advantage of the rights and privileges that belonged to them as children of God. They always were fussing and fighting. Friends, these kinds of things will not only affect your spirit; they'll affect your mind and your body too.

"Love ... takes no account of the evil done to it ...." That has to be the God-kind of love, because Paul says that while we were the enemies of God (Col. 1:21), God didn't take account of the evil done to Him. He loved us and sent Jesus to redeem us. He loved us while we were yet sinners (Rom. 5:8).

"Love ... pays no attention to a suffered wrong ...." "But they did me wrong!" people say. Can't you see that if people walked in love — which is what God wants — it would straighten things out in the home and the church? That's God's answer.

The next verses read, *"It [love] does not rejoice at injustice and unrighteous-*

ness, but rejoices when right and truth prevail. Love bears up under anything and everything that comes...."

Natural human love says, "I just can't take that any longer!" Love can. "I can't put up with that any longer!" Love can.

Sometimes I start thinking about a few situations and I'm prone to get impatient. Then I begin to think about God. He's putting up with all of us. Think about His love, His kindness, and His patience!

The next phrase tells us that love is *"ever ready to believe the best of every person...."* I like this one. Until I read this translation, I didn't know what made me so forgiving, but it was because I listened to the inside of me, and I simply wouldn't let the outside man dominate me.

Some people believe that everybody's out to get them, but love believes the best of every person. It's not God's love that wants to believe the worst about people; natural human love is ready to believe the worst of everyone: the worst about the husband, the worst about the wife, the worst about the children. But this God-kind of love is ever ready to believe the best of every person: husband, wife, children as well as brothers and sisters in the church. (Children believe the best of every person.)

I've followed a policy for approximately 60 years of believing the best of everyone. I don't believe anything bad about anyone.

We traveled through the country for years, holding meetings in churches, and it's amazing how many bad reports we heard. Finally I had to say to some preachers, "I wish you wouldn't talk that way. I'd rather you'd cuss." They were talking about fellow pastors, fellow Christians. It was just something they'd heard. They didn't know whether it was true or not.

You can't go by hearsay. Hearsay won't stand up in court. A lot of people have slop buckets for ears. They run around to hear anything that's bad on anyone. "Oh, have you heard the latest?" they ask. They're sort of gleeful about it.

"Love ... is ever ready to believe the best of every person."

Children ought to have the right to be brought up in this kind of love atmosphere. Then, when they go out into life's fight, they'll win. But when you see the worst in your children, always telling them, "You'll never amount to anything," they'll live up to what you said — they won't amount to anything.

Children make mistakes. You can't put a grown head on a child, so you ought to see the best in them. Work on that. Love them. They will amount to something.

Verse seven concludes by saying that love's *"hopes are fadeless under all circumstances and it endures everything [without weakening]."*

Verse eight reads, *"Love never fails — never fades out or becomes obsolete or comes to an end."*

If you walk in love, you'll never fail.

Love never fails.

Certainly we're interested in spiritual gifts, but *we ought to put love before spiritual gifts.*

Paul went on to say in verse eight that prophecies will fail, tongues will cease, and knowledge will pass away. But, thank God, love never, never, NEVER fails!